Premier Piano Music

Home and Hearth

Contemporary Holiday Solos

Arrangements by

Jacki Alexander

www.PremierPianoMusic.com

Home and Hearth: Contemporary Holiday Solos
Arrangements by Jacki Alexander

Copyright ©2016 Jacki Alexander Music (ASCAP)
Distributed by Premier Piano Music LLC

ISBN : 13 978-1722233785
         10 1722233788

Edited by Jacki Alexander
Printed in the United States of America

Premier Piano Music

PremierPianoMusic.com

Contents
Home and Hearth
Contemporary Holiday Solos

Joy to the World 1

O Come, All Ye Faithful 4

Silent Night 7

Jingle Bells 11

Bring a Torch, Jeanette, Isabella 14

Once in Royal David's City 17

Hanging of the Greens 21

We Three Kings 25

The First Noel 29

Coventry Carol 33

What Child Is This 37

Auld Lang Syne 43

Arrangements by
Jacki Alexander

PremierPianoMusic.com

Joy to the World

George Frideric Handel
Arr. Jacki Alexander

3

O Come, All Ye Faithful

John Francis Wade
Arr. Jacki Alexander

Silent Night

Franz Gruber
Arr. Jacki Alexander

Jingle Bells

James Pierpont
Arr. Jacki Alexander

Swinging

Bring a Torch, Jeanette, Isabella

Traditional French Carol
Arr. Jacki Alexander

Moderately Fast

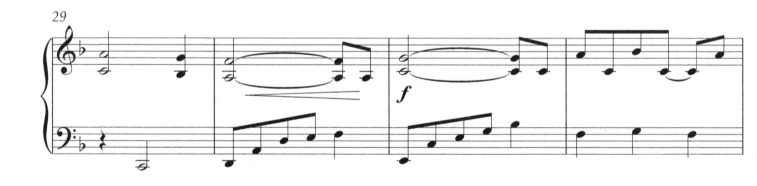

Once in Royal David's City

Henry John Gauntlett
Arr. Jacki Alexander

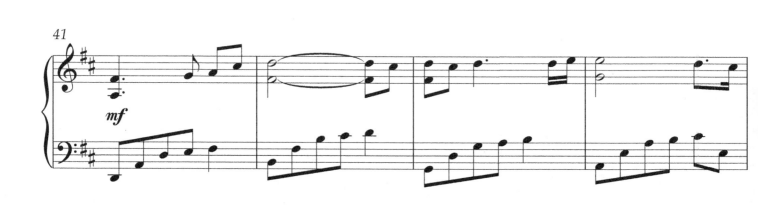

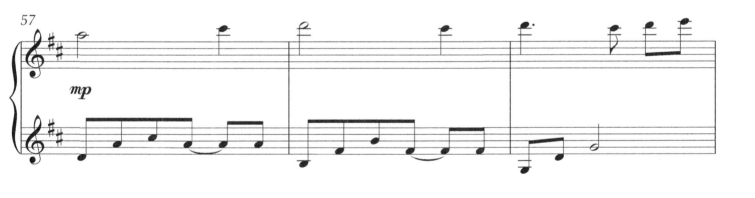

Hanging of the Greens

Medley: Hanging of the Greens/I Saw Three Ships

Traditional
Arr. Jacki Alexander

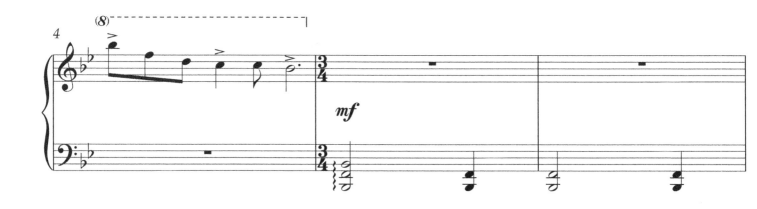

23

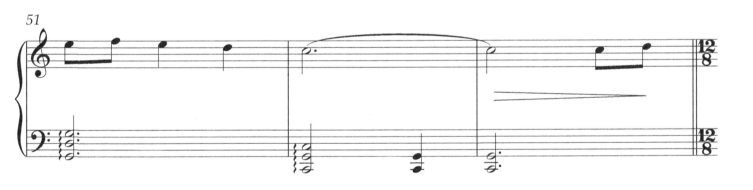

We Three Kings

Jacki Alexander

Moderately

27

The First Noel

Traditional
Arr. Jacki Alexander

Moderately

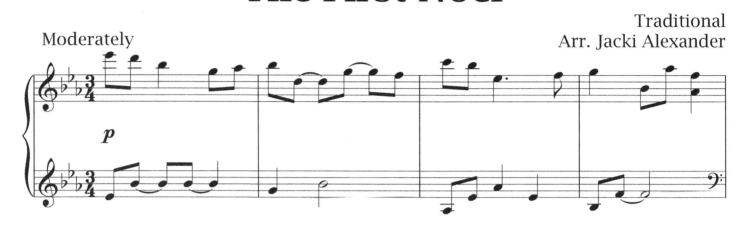

Coventry Carol

Traditional
Arr. Jacki Alexander

Moderately

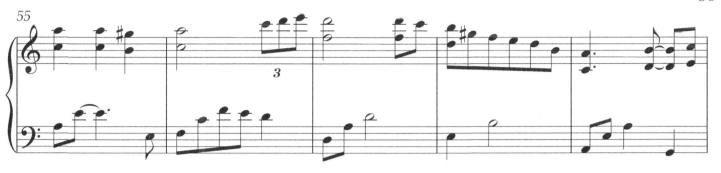

What Child Is This

Traditional
Arr. Jacki Alexander

Moderately

poco rit.　　　　　a tempo

L.H.

bring out melody

poco rit.

a tempo

L.H.

mf

Auld Lang Syne

Traditional
Arr. Jacki Alexander

Moderately

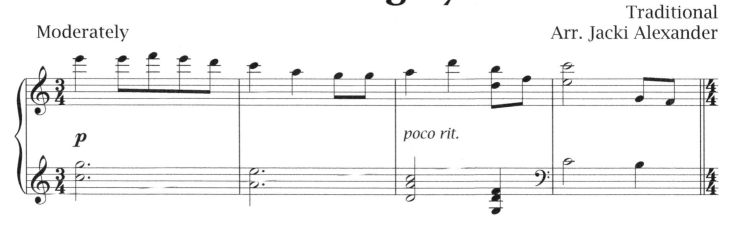

bring out melody

www.premierpianomusic.com

Made in the USA
Coppell, TX
30 October 2021